Praise for *The l*

GW00676528

"Very Insightful read. I expect my granddaughter will be considered as a candidate for the priesthood!"

—Belva Kohler, Proud Catholic grandmother and
sponsor of her granddaughter for Confirmation

"Fr. Jim has been a prophetic voice calling for the inclusion of women in the Church. It is not radical feminist theology. It is simply Gospel truth. We are all made in God's image and the Church would fulfill its mission better if it embraced completely all the gifts of God's female children."

—Ken Cooper - Theology Teacher, St. John's High School,
Washington, DC

"Beautifully written and honest. Formed from decades of service to college students in the South Bronx, Jim's prophetic vision is necessary and is to be blessed—the sooner the better—regarding the role of women in public, priestly service."

—Padre Nelson Belizario, Ph.D., OCarm

"In this collection of short meditations, veteran New York City priest James Sheehan celebrates women he has had the privilege of getting to know over his many years of life and pastoral ministry. None of the women we meet in these delightful vignettes are conventionally famous or powerful; but, as Sheehan's recollections reveal, all of them are followers of the Gospel who have made a difference in his life, in the lives of their families and neighbors, and in the life of the Church writ large. Writing with his signature verve and robust humanity, Fr. Sheehan invites us to encounter the wholesome holiness of just a few of the millions of flesh-and-blood women who make up the true substance of the church as the Body of Christ. Sheehan's reverent respect for these ordinary but extraordinary women undergirds as well his prophetic challenge to the Catholic Church that he and they have served with such loyalty and grace: to reform currently-restrictive Church teaching and practice so that in the future, women's gifts can be fully exercised in all areas of its leadership and life."

—Christine Firer Hinze, Professor, Theological and Social Ethics, Fordham University

"This is a superb collection of insightful and incisive portraits of women and their relationships with their faith and a Catholic priest. Walking beside Father Jim Sheehan on this thought-provoking and poignant journey, we lament the Church's failure to model respect for women in leadership and its decision to ignore and devalue the many gifts they could share to build a more loving, peaceful and just world."

—Carolyn Kost, Feminist and Former Professor of Religious Studies

"When will the men in power realize that the women have left the Garden of Eden a long time ago — and can lead."

—Sister Margaret Treacy, RSHM,
International Missioner and Educator

"Jim Sheehan is one of the best feminists I know. He is a man who refuses to stay on the sidelines as women are over-looked for life-giving care in the Catholic Church. Instead he 'releases whatever he has left (and there is plenty left that I can testify to)' to the universe for a long recognition that could give care as compassionately as men—maybe more so—having been deprived of the opportunity for too long."

—Ruth Wooden, MA, Director, Encore Transitional Program,
Union Theological Seminary

"Reverend James Sheehan's love of the women in his life resonates through every page of what reads like a love letter to sacred companions. These are women who wear life like a loose garment, and navigate the alternating seasons with reverential grief and joy. Raised as a Protestant in a highly conservative Baptist tradition, I never imagined the Catholic tradition becoming an integral part of my ongoing spiritual formation. I have Reverend Jim to thank in part for expanding my lens on the mysterious wonder of spiritual practices birthed from worlds of Catholic mothers and fathers. Reverend Jim's sacred friendship and ministerial partnership with college students has companioned and affirmed me in ways that keep me on the Way. I give thanks to the women, like Reverend's Jim's mother. They teach him to serve as a "midwife" for women on the Way."

—Carolyn Harrison, Bronx Director of Young Life, an Evangelical Christian Outreach to Youth

"Fr. Sheehan has written 12 charming vignettes about strong women he has known across the decades. He presents them almost in situ, as their lives entered into his own life. He does this without loading weighty analysis upon who they are, what they were, how they changed across the years. He simply states and nears witness to who they are, and appreciates what they meant to him."

—Donna B. Doucette, Executive Director, Voice of the Faithful

"The twelve vibrant and unvarnished portraits of faithful women whose stories inspire Roman Catholic priest, Fr. James Coy Sheehan, in this book, *The Unfinished Table* are a joy to read. Fr. Sheehan's friends include a triathlon-running nurse now doctor; an Irish International educator; and a Spanish-speaking immigrant college student. Some of these women are practicing Catholics. Some are working mothers. None are ordained Roman Catholic priests. Sheehan's pithy and delightful conversations with women whose struggles, laughter and ambitions are all-so-human, remind us that real men of the cloth are called to listen. And here is a question poised between the pages: Are the priestly gift of ALL people called for in such a time as this?"

—Reverend Chloe Breyer

"An inspirational book of godly women whose voices are lacking from our Catholic pulpit."

—Father Thomas Fenlon, Senior Priest,
Archdiocese of New York

"Father Jim Sheehan has a singularly enjoyable approach highlighting the journeys and faith statements of several women who have influenced his own spirituality in this book. He has written each testimony with full and vulnerable transparency, which allows readers to connect with each woman on a deep level. Every story is unique in context and experience. They will encourage others to gain strength and wisdom to meet daily struggles with an open heart and their prophetic voice."

—Ashley W.

THE UNFINISHED TABLE

12 WOMEN WHO AFFECT MY LIFE JOURNEY

The Unfinished Table: 12 Woman Who Affect My Life Journey
Copyright © 2022 Rev. James Sheehan

COY Publishing Company

All rights reserved. No part of this book may be reproduced (except for inclusion in reviews), disseminated, or utilized in any form or by any means, electronic or mechanical, including photocopying, recording, or in any information storage and retrieval system, or the Internet/World Wide Web without written permission from the author or publisher.

Book design by:
Arbor Services, Inc.
www.arborservices.co/

Printed in the United States of America

The Unfinished Table: 12 Woman Who Affect My Life Journey
Rev. James Sheehan

1. Title 2. Author 3. Spiritual / Faith

Library of Congress Control Number: 2021921173
ISBN 13: 978-0-578-31017-6

THE UNFINISHED TABLE

12 WOMEN WHO AFFECT MY LIFE JOURNEY

REV. JAMES SHEEHAN

DEDICATED TO THOSE WHO DREAM

Contents

Forward

There is no shortage of female figures in scripture, but the spotlight is rarely upon them. Most Christians will be familiar with some of the stories of the matriarchs like Sarah, Rebecca, Rachel, and Leah, and certainly Mary, the mother of Jesus. These women model faithfulness and service and reveal an important role that goes beyond the identities of their husbands and sons. Mothers are revered in scripture for good reason. At great personal sacrifice and the risk of their own death in childbirth, women have courageously partnered with the divine to ensure human survival, to model God's love, and to teach children to live a godly life.

Women ensure the continuity of traditions connecting religion with ethnic belonging and customs through food, like the Italian feast of the seven fishes, Polish wigilia, French réveillon, and Mexican rosca de reyes. Women undoubtedly prepared the Passover seder that was likely Jesus' last meal with his disciples, but we are not permitted to preside over its reenactment at Mass. Only men can be ordained to the Catholic priesthood, even though the bible tells us that Mary Magdalene was the first to preach the good news of the resurrection.

In stark contrast, the vast majority of female Catholic saints were not mothers. They devoted themselves to pastoral works, charity, and prayer, defended the faith and often suffered horrible fates for their virtue. The model they provide is most often one of self-sacrifice and selflessness. And that needs further examination. Catholicism is not alone among religions in identifying sin with pride, self-assertion, and hunger for power, but these are more commonly men's sins. Women's sins would be rightfully characterized as dependence on others, lack of self and boundaries, and the privileging of the needs of their own children over those of others or the common good. Those sins don't make it into any examination of conscience I've ever seen precisely because the experience of men is centered as a matter of course when men are at the center.

Regardless, ordained or not, the priesthood of the believer is real, and prophets, those who challenge the status quo as spokespersons for God and energize us toward a better alternative, exist, and in both cases sex is irrelevant. The Church is God's people; it is no more anti-woman than the broader society, but probably not much less either. To tell stories, as scripture does, to help us to see what we have overlooked, that is the task of prophets, among them Father Jim Sheehan.

Jim calls us to consider the women who have accompanied him on his faith journey. There are caretakers with quiet fortitude, feisty tellers of the unvarnished truth, and mothers who birth babies, projects and ideas. These are women who have presence, who challenge and befriend Mystery, and with whom you will want to share the sacrament of friendship at the table, so pull up a chair and listen.

Carolyn Kost
Thanksgiving, 2021

Introduction

Why Write?

Here I sit with a sloppy table full of memories about life during the slow death of COVID that has stabbed in my heart all my ways of being in relationship.

Gone even are my routines which I once found so irritating!

I described myself this week to another priest as deflated. I am not prone to self-pity, but COVID hurts. To see too many friends not die, but slowly drift away from family events, meals and baseball games hurt badly.

Really, is a guy from the Bronx to get excited about black-and-white Korean baseball on YouTube?

What about deaths that might occur shortly for relatives that moved to Florida to soak in the sun and play golf? They are not in nursing homes yet — the new Petri dishes of death as they are now called. I expect a cell-phone telephone or a professional e-mail rudely announcing death soon. I still remember the phone call on a landline on a black rotary phone call in a pre-air conditioned summer in the Bronx apartment house of my youth when some cousin called my mother.

Mom always was the first one the family called — or so it seemed. She seemed to handle harsh news calmly, publicly, and intelligently.

She gently did this even though her heart was often burdened with yet another sign that some things could not be changed —no matter how much one prays nor studies nor wishes it were different.

The non-existent cheers are calling the last game.

The dishes in the sink and the stale chips from last night simply state the obvious; we do not feel there is much space for living, nor dancing, nor laughing anymore, nor even writing – or so it seems.

Our tears are dried up.

So we — or I — write to release what energy I have left to the universe. There might be a few others like you who do want to travel with me on the aging # 1 train and find out where we are heading.

I want to share some stammering from my heart about the sacred, imperfect people who brought me to a felt consciousness of the Higher Power. I hope against hope that my own doubts are the very springboard to some kind of faith and purpose in life.

I will write about women for they are involved in birthing in a lonely planet that cries out for touch even when it is not allowed. I write because they function more than the receivers of news of death – as they do take steps and giggles that breathe new life. I write about them because they still pray loudly through their whispers of their own truths at what keeps themselves in churches that do not want to use their gifts openly and fairly.

Maybe I write about women because without them I would not be the man that I am today. I am facing some decline in body and soul at 68 in a 2,000 year old, creaking system. The institution that I work for over four decades is clearly cracking under the weight of too many storms. The tragic result is a neglected chilling of the brains and hearts and even souls.

I write because I need to tell the truth. This precious truth cannot be controlled; prayerfully, it will bring fire onto the inertia and wet blankets that have smothered the renewed intercourse that is the life of the Spirit in a dark world.

I write because the telling of the story needs to be stated.

The audience and the future is not as important as myself – my own audience — hearing the phone calls and e-mails that proclaim life as well as death, the real stuff that even COVID cannot strip away. This naturally includes the loving embrace from women companions. They still skip across the thin space from even physical death with much life at the Breaking of the Bread—and yes, a shared glass of wine can help.

Why would I dare wait until further deaths by COVID come to the world that once was so secure?

No.

Let us get the food on the table and the homework done.

Women are waiting.

Chapter 1

Ann

She sure did not look particularly pious or religious, as she sat in her jeans with holes in them and a glass of white wine in her thin hands. She was sitting comfortably on the edge of a worn-family sofa in an otherwise well-appointed home. If there were any family secrets, the only one that surprised me was that she actually had become a grandmother of eleven since we had last met.

But she needed to talk about death.

In some way, she was beginning to join herself to the pyramid builders of Egypt and to her Baptist parents, and now her closest woman friend, who had died suddenly.

She, a retired teacher, was also a knowledgeable, and thus an almost inevitably frustrated Catholic. She had entered the Roman Church through what was the new program of the RCIA (Rite of Christian Initiation of Adults) in her suburban Southern parish. This positive experience was shaped by a fine priest who had gone to my seminary. He had introduced us thirty-eight years ago, and

1

had softly mentioned to me in a visit the suggestion that I would enjoy her and her family.

He was right.

She did not stand on ceremony, and we still laugh with gusto at her jumping over the furniture in her home so as not to disturb the toys and forts of her children.

He had spoken the truth at many levels. We do wonder about his whereabouts as he has long since left the priesthood to get married and start his own family. As only a happy mother who is still in love with her family could say: "That rule of celibacy is just plain out and out silly!"

She wanted now to plan her funeral, a strange request in a pleasant mid-summer evening. Her interest in death was not morbid, nor prompted by a secret disease.

To be sure, she wanted to make things simple for her family one more time. Graying around the temples of the forehead, she manifested a real, burning desire to learn what the Mass and prayers could offer her family at this significant inevitable time of transition.

Why would one ever allow the Liturgy to be impersonal, or cold?

She was still feeling the pain of her neighbors and the family of a close friend who had died at the same age as herself, a young in spirit grandmother like herself.

Energy is an intrinsic part of her life, and that is precisely why she was in conflict with her local parish.

She was not content to being "the last one in the parish under seventy years of age." She deeply desired for the religious enterprise to be part and parcel of getting the family to enjoy and celebrate well their time together. She had committed her family to this quest on a regular basis; thus it was natural that her granddaughter had asked her to be her sponsor for Confirmation.

A simple request, but there was conflict with the local parish structure, led by a stubborn traditionalist pastor. Belva Ann being Belva Ann had been in so much conflict with him that several of her friends and family prudently encouraged not to go to her parish. She flew her wings, and found a Mass on Zoom with a modern priest friend. Belva Ann and her husband had married as teens right after high school, and they could now be at peace while celebrating and praying together with a small, loyal and intelligent community on Zoom. She, and her granddaughter, got the letter of sponsorship from her priest friend.

The future of faith for her is a bit like Abraham's gazing into the brightness of the uncountable stars. Her faithful love of the family is real, and yet, not enmeshed. As she swims, laughs and prays for the freedom of her family, she will not be held back by any gloom and doom.

So, as both the Baptist and Catholic Bible states so succinctly:

"O death, where is your victory, where is your sting?" (1 Corinthians 15:55)

Chapter 2

Maggie

WHICH PART DO YOU CHOOSE?

As she bounced in late to class again after working in the age of printed, non-digital yearbooks, I did see there were many aspects of this teen that I would never figure out. Was it her evident feistiness, although she was distinctly polite? Was it her fragility which she readily admitted, even after starting a long-distance runners' club before it was fashionable? Was it her deep faithfulness, even though the winds of change around women's issues were stirring even then in her and her peers?

She touched many bases in her international background of being the youngest daughter of a car-testing, blue-collar father, who had found international work in the mountains of Switzerland. She moved from there with her family to being an enthusiastic, wide-eyed student with other smart girls in Rome. Next came a jaunt to the USA to study in a Jesuit university. At 17, this was the *first* time that she actually lived in the USA. Conditioned by many real, finely-chiseled and disciplined middle-class values, she loved nursing. She learned her communication skills with hospital personnel from her upbringing with two solid believing parents and by visiting patients as a nurse, not from medical school. She also quickly saw that as a natural stepping stone to being an M.D. All that focused enthusiasm evolved into being a pediatrician married to another doctor, whom she had met in a sprawling, impersonal university. She had, and has standards. This meant there was no frivolous time spent at the big, nationally televised football games, where there was too much drinking and alcohol abuse for her tastes. Her three adult children can attest to her high standards, except when it came *to cooking!*

Her mind kept her from buying any package too readily.

Being self-reflective, she knew that the medical and ecclesial institutions that she was connected with were simply too big and too entrenched to deal with the human dilemma of brokenness. Pregnancies abounded with mothers of the children she served as a hardworking pediatrician. Neither the Church, which she wanted to respect, nor the medical institutions, was able to touch the real issues of self-image and bills that had to be paid. She looked to create community where she worked. This woman and doctor still knows both intuitively and experientially that corporate agendas from on-high could be dangerous to the health of her soul and that of her co-workers.

Her running outdoors, even on her shaky and injured knees, clearly proclaims to her different worlds that this thin woman is strong. Running fiercely and so well in triathlons more than once allowed her to get to know herself outside the expected roles of a woman in a small town in the 21st century.

Her soul is both private and social. She does alertly engage other folks to some point of self-awareness, expecting that they themselves can push themselves across the finish line.

This soul makes time to be filled with meditation. She drove long distances to be with her ailing and aging Italian-Swiss patriarchal father so as to look at a calming lake with him. On Sundays, she often bicycles to hear the birds again and again. Like the wide-eyed student of life that she is, she wonders: "Where does all this beauty come from?" She continues her search for viable truths. Naturally flustered by the sheer refusal of both sides of the political aisle to admit that the medical system is terribly broken, she keeps moving and darting between very real obstacles put in her way.

She will not be stopped.

Although the object of her faith is fuzzier than where she first began with a defined religion, she understands very well the need for a wider vision that she sees as touching her concrete realities.

She wants to find quality family time;

She desires to find quality conversations;

And she still expects herself not to be made a big deal of even as she articulates well the pains of those who are not heard in systems at conferences and hallways in Washington and state capitols.

Long ago, her voice has left that of church halls and sacristies. That is a shame; this is sadly a tale repeated by so many other women who were educated by the religiously motivated schools.

The female bearers of the future have often drifted away, sometimes from anger and often from boredom. Without them, even the stones and half-empty pews cry out: "No more new life!"

However, her own faithfulness to some inner, shy voice still cries out for more intelligent discussion of women's rights, much more than strident rhetoric.

Her faithfulness is also given clearly and freely to her family. Her interest and connection to her siblings both here and in the next dimension really is amazing. Whatever fragility she may have had with her body has been forced to be forgotten by her friends ages ago; she does not allow that to be the center of who she is.

Her identity also is involved in trying to understand others, more accurately to stand under them as they run or stumble on their own life-journey. Her eyes observe much, but her mouth is often quiet as her sees life-decisions being worked out—time and time again.

As the glow of a setting sun can be fuzzy at the end of a cross-country run, her way of being might even appear a bit hazy. However, her gentle spirit is not split.

This woman's birthing of a new, more equal world is multi-dimensional, which is strong, wiry, and nuanced. Her intelligent approaches into mundane reality really do challenge all. Perhaps, the complexity of her inner life actually invites others to try to capture her by one aspect of her personality. All of those attempts are silly and a waste of time. She is not to be pinned down, nor controlled.

Her running is not primarily to take her away from arbitrary controls, but does involve making a path where none have been before.

Good for her; good for us.

Chapter 3

Emma

Wow — no need for a middle name for her.

She was huge and dominating woman at 6 foot, 4 inches tall. She was intimidating to many folks, including her son and the other physically-fit civil service men in the family. Her first husband had died in the migration from Boston to the West Side of Manhattan.

Uncle Arthur, her brother and gruff cigar-chomping New York City Fire Captain was somehow able to penetrate her hard shell. My dad did well enough with her when she was his boss when he came from Chicago to New York in the drama of the Irish American diaspora. The family joke was Aunt Emma was so tough and demanding at Schraff's factory in Manhattan to drive him into the "easy job" of putting out fires as a fireman.

She got re-married, and the second husband also died!

I am not sure what her spirituality was.

She officially was Episcopalian, which stood out as exceptional when she moved to Inwood that was *very* Roman Catholic, and Irish Catholic at that. She lived for the future—as she loved the trips to what we considered the wilds of New City across the Tappan Zee Bridge to visit her three granddaughters.

The soft underbelly of Emma's drive to put her success-driven face on the family appeared when she was sick at the old dormitory space for patients at the huge, impersonal Columbia Presbyterian Hospital in Washington Heights.

Uncle Arthur would sneak in with fresh cherries for his ill sister. This was probably one of the first hospital visits that I ever made when I was allowed above the lobby to the wards and the large dormitories of the mid-'60's . The collusion of law-abiding Aunt Emma and Uncle Arthur made them accessible, human, even enriching visits —so unlike many visits to the bed-ridden in our high-tech worlds.

Then there was her stubbornness.

She was determined to be alive and thus able to attend my Priestly Ordination at Saint Patrick's Cathedral. We all were grateful that her hearing was gone by the time when the Church called James FRANCIS Sheehan to the High Altar, and *not* James COY Sheehan. Coy was her family name. She would have been very annoyed with the high mucky-mucks who merely used my saint's name for Confirmation, and not HER family name!

Silence was NOT a virtue of hers.

Another unusual side of her would show up. This was her wild curiosity in how children were being raised, which she often disapproved of; what people were having for dinner; and what was going on in the electronic Church from the Crystal Cathedral! She would have her evening prayer of a Manhattan, and then would call my mother Helen to ask her what she was having for dinner.

She did outlive all women in the family—and with a glint-in-the-eye, would recommend her type of holy water.

Every-so-often, Mom would try to tell Emma that she was cooking for her fire-department husband and two boys. Yes; she was busy in the apartment house's small kitchen! That did not really matter to Emma; she just presumed that she had every right to know what the ingredients were that evening for the quasi-sacramental nature of a regular sit-down meal.

Can I use the word, "Mystery" for what made this formidable woman tick with her God?

It sure was neither vulnerability nor humility.

She was proud to be a different kind of woman, and could care less about anyone understanding or daring to minimize her determination to keep her family safe and solid in her mind. Emma, like Esther and Judith in their sly ways in the Hebrew Scriptures, often got her way too.

Chapter 4

Anne

Is she really, the simple straight-shooting "second cousin once removed," or someone much more complicated?

She found me on the Internet when she sent me an e-mail saying "Don't delete me." This often leads to being deleted. I am glad that I opened her mail, an almost radical act of faith reflecting our common need to be in contact with someone in our digitally challenged and fragmented world.

Separation was not an option in family life when we grew up.

Somewhere in the end of the pre-air-conditioned summer, Mom, Dad, my brother and myself went in the old Buick "All the way up" across the old Tappan Zee Bridge to New City and the booming hamlets in New City area. Unknown to my brother and myself, Anne, the oldest of three sisters, and her family really looked with enthusiasm to the city cousins making the trek. To be sure, it was a command performance expected by the dominant Aunt Emma of family lore.

The visit was to happen—and it happened.

13

So maybe, I need not have been surprised by the e-mail from Anne.

She was going back to a high school reunion in old suburbia. We saw each other on a Saturday morning. On Saturday afternoon, I was teaching in a working class college made up of students who had dropped out of college, or had never gone to college.

The worlds of that Saturday and schools could not have been more different than our families' experience regarding education. We both had families that were fully "into education." The family legends include as a central point the day when Anne was called into the principal's office. Her clearly Protestant mother had her dressed in an orange sweater as the public high school was celebrating Irish culture around the feast of Patrick.

She became a medical technologist, and returned to college as a serious art student at 52. The driven quest for knowledge was in her blood; it was what diligent middle-class families expected for their children, even in the turbulent '60s.

Her family in what we called upstate was clearly Protestant. For all the discussion of religion as a family staple, no one really explained what either Protestant or Catholic meant to the children. We knew they were Protestant; they knew we were Roman Catholic, which meant that they were not Roman Catholic.

There was bonding though in other ways though, as her state trooper father helped fixed my brother's baseball bat. He and his oldest daughter, a tomboy of that period, loved going to Yankee Stadium in the still unchanged Bronx.

Fast forward to the age of e-mail, I now daily encounter images of an iconic woman, my once distant cousin. Lean in frame, she rightly can be compared to a "mighty fortress is our God." She continually chooses to be herself in the midst of changing times, particularly with marriage, raising three children and being a medical technologist. However, the pragmatic, roughly hewn family fortress has been cruelly challenged.

She had left her medical career in a career change at 52. She wanted to leave the rat-race, and she did! She established a pottery barn at the age of 60 to make jars for the tourists as they came to Amish land in Ohio. For seven or so years, all seemed apparently idyllic. But for the last ten years her life has been poured out, as surely as water spilling out through a cracked jar. Her strong husband, a businessman and volunteer swim instructor, became a hemiplegic, with significant paralysis. When he is not in a wheel-chair, he regularly falls out of bed. His wife knows the emergency team of the local fire department all too well. Her mother-in-law became more ill and moved in. After much cajoling from some loved ones, Anne moved again and now lives with her ill family in a smaller house near her daughter.

How does she handle all these back-breaking and heart wrench-ing chores is beyond me, but the courageous discipline of "showing up on time" continues.

Every morning, in cold-to-the-bone winter and through the warm, humid days of rural Ohio summers, she slows down, reads or meditates. Then, almost automatically, she tries to communicate in short e-thoughts with a few others, including myself. This occurs like clockwork near 7:20 AM. In no way is this a plea for pity, and it is not a prayer from the dark night of the soul. The e-mail is her matter of fact description of the grueling day that she puts in as part and parcel of being married. I know fully well that here is much grounded love waiting to burst into the open as death is looming nearer, but the only sign that change is happening is the e-mail now come to me closer to 8:20 AM. Although unstated, what is painfully obvious is that there are more accidents and deterioration to take care of.

She is not a warm fuzzy; she does not have to be. Her straight-forwardness is what is helping her family now, as it has before.

No one knows how she does it, and others and I have wondered about that before. For herself, she seems not to care where her real strength comes from.

Her duty is before her—and she shows up.

If she gives credit to any source for this strength, it is directed to vivid memories of learning these values at her grandmother's knees. Yes; those come from the almost mystical Aunt Emma.

Is that not what good people do? Show up!

Her witness whispers crosses over physical distance. This staunch silent service definitely speaks louder than her real shortness of words and very limited use of the phone.

The home of her solid family life has been cracked more than once, and it *continues* to crumble. However, whatever engaging truth lies in family ties that prompted her to make that web search and found me still makes sense. The deep healing sense and expectations from the elders helps us to create opportunities to do the impossible in a daily, non-begrudging way.

While the health scenes are urgent, she *does* calmly respond in a calm, almost baffling simple sense of service.

How does she do it?

She has no interest in the apron strings of religion.

How DOES she do it?

The vows that she took in New York State forty plus years ago are very fresh.

The vows are to be kept.

Bending over for her fallen husband again, she may curse that truth, but they show up.

She would have it no other way.

The starkness of her commitment is like Calvary without the Good Friday rituals.

Her witness haunts me.

Chapter 5

Ellen and Eternal Energy

It was her youthful laugh that invited me.

A heart-felt healthy laugh at all the incomplete angles of her life. She never stopped believing in the real importance of the values from her real small town where she came from. Her homespun values were often in sharp contrast to the opaque worlds that appeared in the digitized offices of the corporate world and the churches, which she served so diligently.

She was not to be controlled, and from early on no one was to get in the way of her love of nature. She found her God in many venues. She really appreciated religious practitioners who did not try to push one school of spirituality, denomination, or tradition upon her.

To do that was a waste of time anyway. Her God was wider than any one way of doing things, and she was always hopeful that her home team of Catholicism would be open to the ordination of women and of married men. She claimed the Holy Spirit in all paths of life, including cancer.

That dreaded disease is what she physically died from after a long thirteen years from the initial diagnosis. Yes; she was annoyed at the Western medicines that did things to her beautiful body. She willingly accepted natural healing herbs, unlike the "wicked Western medicines" which I and others from overseas insisted that she take. We will have no way of knowing what worked or didn't work, but she was not about death, but of life.

She blessed life, and was blessed by life itself. Without her, the sunrise Easter Liturgies would never have had happened. The folks who made it to the East River Park, not far from the dog-ramble, were as Raggedy-Ann as the first bunch of out of breath women and scared apostles at the empty cave. A rock had been moved, "Where did they put Our Lord?..." stammered the women.

We do not know.

And maybe never will.

However, we can look for him as she did in the rekindling of friendships and the shared joy that can occur with the wine which she loved. For all her interest in the emotional, she loved books. By no means was this an isolated venue to pick up esoteric wisdom, but it served as a way to share the insights with other women in one of her many book clubs. Truth was a shared venture for her.

She loved Christmas in a uniquely celebratory way. She would have no troubles listening to Mahalia Jackson sing Christmas carols through all hours of the night. This was a darkness that would be lit by candles until she could embrace the dawn. She was not fatigued by her all-nighter, and she eagerly looked forward to entertaining her friends of all kinds and sections of her New York world. Her well-appointed banquet table would include a Jewish woman, a Holocaust survivor, from her university evenings after work; a Venezuelan businesswoman who had shared unemployment with her; a Polish Catholic gymnast turned massage therapist; my friend, the lanky, quiet man who expressed thanksgiving all the time; and myself, who never could believe that punctuality was important as spending oodles of time with her.

The laughter that often burst out came naturally from her; her quiet pride radiated that she could graciously set out a meal and enjoy it herself. The laughter touched all corners of her studio apartment. Small though she was, she loomed big in everybody's consciousness. Her tiny kitchen was filled with an expansive, heart-warming love.

The holiday was never complete without her warm family of five checking on each other. Each of the three brothers and one sister looked forward to calling her, the youngest. She, beginning with punch cards and a solid work-ethic, had done well in New York City in the new field of computer programming.

She was not to be controlled by one continent and she had a deep friendship with her girlfriend in Munich. They were almost like twins in their physical beauty in their bikinis and miniskirts of their young working days, and their spiritual sensitivity to all aspects of the cosmos and nature. Far from being staid, both of them could enjoy their girly, international conversations by phone cards on Saturday mornings. They joyfully enjoyed remembering tales of their apparently wild beach vacations and cruises, where even smoking cigarettes and shared glasses of wine were beginning to be quite the rage for working single women in the changing times of the '60s. She continued her respect for modernity by having four sockets for electronic gizmos in the studio apartment, not all of which were connected to her job.

Spirituality, the ability to breathe, came naturally to her, often in front of mountains. Looming large in snapshots were mountains, such as Machu Picchu in Peru, the Alps outside of Munich with her German friend having mulled wine; and the smaller yet equally significant hills in her deeply beloved Poconos near her vacation and retirement home.

She retreated to this last site often. Her humble house there was a warm, open-air palace to friends, family and neighbors. Then there was the extra dimension as the deer would show up with their doleful and soulful eyes looking for food. Both the fawns and their parents knew that she appreciated them, and she would only serve healthy food.

⭧ ⭧ ⭧

I was in Rome when I was notified that she died. A sincere e-mail from a friend and co-worker from the early days of her business-woman career announced it. This was clear, stark and awful. I kept moving as stillness was impossible.

A good taxista (cabbie) explained to me that the concerto of music that I was going to was actually in the Anglican Church of Saint Paul's Within the Walls. This was not Saint Paul's Outside the

Walls, where Saint Pope John XXIII in 1958 called for the opening of Vatican II to help the Roman Church to become updated and help the modern world. "Fine; va bene," I muttered. The ticket collector in the Anglican version saw my pain, and my inability to use the computer system to print out a ticket. He let me in for nothing. I appreciated the religious music, both comforting and compelling. I also appreciated the Irish bar and restaurant nearby, as I watched European football to turn my focus away from my pain.

The funeral was to wait until I got home; I will swear she had arranged her death that way. She did not want me to see her suffer, even while in a fine hospice on the Upper East Side of Manhattan.

So I went early the next morning to Assisi, the town of Francis which she loved. I also made it to Florence, the city of art and love. This city nestled in the Umbrian Hills touches all things and all times with needed beauty and the fullness of the soul, and what it means to be really alive.

What else can you say about a city that has a sculpture of the poet Dante right outside a Church? The Florentines knew that art is not far from the pearly gates of love and thus heaven. They still know that art invites us into the heart of being human.

I could feel her gentle gaze emanating from her eyes. They were often swelling with emotions and tears of passion, warmth and strength, simply stating to me: "Keep it simple." I tried to do that as I saw the unkempt shirt of a teenage female worker in a bookstore with a quotation in Italian from the Divine Comedy. Very loosely translated, it goes something like this: "Love never lets you go."

True. The pain in "relationship," her favorite word, is worth it. Every last, and first bit of it. All of it. So true. Thank you to the big-city woman from a small town, for making space for us. Small towns, small apartments and the expansive sanctuary of your heart would not have had it any other way.

Chapter 6

Josephine

Or is that, "Jo, as in Jo?"

I met her as simple and straightforward, sitting on the edge of a cold chair in a half-empty retreat house, now closed, near the border of the north of Ireland. She was energetically concerned to hear the things of the Spirit, dying to hear and see and feel the new face of God.

As a farm girl, she drove a tractor at the young age of 15. Her hands and heart are still strong.

Her skills and her heart are like silent, almost cold steel driven down firmly in the soil of a devout, and yet realistic view of Church. This includes its figures with feet of clay in this horrendous age of the pedophilia scandals.

Far from covering up the real failings of the Church on earth, she reveals a real physical blinking in her eyes as she creates an alternative community of the beloved disciples around her Lady of Knock. She knows one gets there only by sloughing along the unpolished pilgrimage rocks around Lough Derg both really and symbolically.

Her prayer is tied into song, a lilt on words, warm and rich family memories, amidst the economically challenged realities of County Monagahan. The possibilities of entrance into the modern world were stymied by the changing of the different gauge for the British trains going to the north, leaving Monaghan City only able to serve the south. Her type of faith roots her and invites her forward.

She has prayed the ancient daily discipline of the rosary on her knees for years. She has prayed intensely for her wanderlust daughter who works at the international scenes of humanitarian service at dangerous sites, and her home-bird husband. He hardly leaves the home base except when he gets called to read their poetry and short-stories with his wife on radio. Often unvoiced, she has an intense, humble connection with other family members and neighbors, who have had more difficult lives than her own.

Her Lord is not to be held captive, and she understands that the world has changed. She and her well-married husband knew that to greet the future they needed to depict the well-bonded communities of rural Ireland with vivid short stories to capture their original embers of love in THEIR backwoods section of the Emerald Isle. They have thus written a fine book about their rural Ireland, full of good short-stories of villages – way before the global village. Today is a whole new ballgame. She is concerned for the still-cold, stultifying Church life that has blighted the community — as if the potato famine has returned with vengeance.

She has seen beyond that, and was comfortable arranging her marriage to be blessed in romantic Rome. The marriage has lasted a good, long time.

Jo is in touch with her life-journey, and the real-limits of some neighbors and long-simmering— and often silly feuds. She is not to be bogged down by the mud of inertia that seems to be the way of much of the life of a small town. Although her petite body can be found in the drafty area of a large Cathedral Church, she is not of it. Hers is not a small minded, stiff upper-lip form of religion that has coldly looked with a real fatalism at the depression and alcohol-abuse that still plagues many families.

In her clever, non-judgmental way of traveling on the religious quest, she walks almost a *via negativa* trail avoiding that which is NOT of the free, life-giving, heartfelt blessings of the Lord. She slips away from the sins of sitting on the Holy Spirit.

She is NOT naive, but keeps her opinions to herself. When she trusts a representative of the Church, her thoughts do come out gushing like a river creating new rivulets in the already damp ground that can become bog-like.

Although she is connected to the religious package that still is Irish Catholicism, and does many of the same rituals that her mother did, she expands by reading and choosing to penetrate some of the creation spirituality and poetry of John O'Donohue. She walks lightly and nervously on the shaky reality that many good priests who see beyond the rituals have left – or have been forced out by the institutional side of a cold, defensive failing and imploding system.

She is not scared of the future, although is naturally concerned for the youth, and her priest-friends, who live often, needlessly lonely lives.

She captures – more than most – that Gospel-quest to be in the world and not of it. Between her quick steps and her knowledge of the backroads and even highways in her small car near her town, she intends to go out and meet the living, enfleshed Lord.

I was with her once at a parish cemetery once – old, rugged, and foreboding—except for her gentle words. Jo explained as well as she could the lives, the struggles and deaths of her neighbors and friends of the Lord. She was not over-whelmed by death at all. Just like the women on the early first Easter morn, she had moved the rocked, cragged rocks outside the Tomb.

In the Lord, she has an old trusted friend.

With a glint in her earnest eyes, she quietly and firmly intends to have a real conversation over good, hot tea with the Lady of Knock. When the Lady of Knock appeared with the Apostle John and the poor, this Mother said NOTHING.

The fellows were to know what a lady like Mary and Jo wants, desires, and yes, expects.

Chapter 7

Margaret

Her internationalism began small—very small.

Where in God's good name is Locust Gap, Pennsylvania, the little town where she was born?

There lies a coal-mining town with strong mix of Irish and German blood mixing together to remind folks that the only way out is education. Her mother died at too young of an age, and her prayers to Mary with rosary on her knees were tied into this profound absence. Limited though they were, the family came through as best they could. She was glad to go to a Catholic Girls' High School in Brooklyn.

The Spirit works where She will.

After she had gone as a sophomore to a weekday Mass, the math teacher— a sister – asked a significant question to the students.

Well, at least my friend heard this heart-felt question:

"What if it's all true? The Eucharist that is …that God really does come to us at the Mass?"

This simple declarative question did not go away in her many venues of service. These include the days of a very crowded novitiate in a well-off section of Connecticut to its closing of the nursing facility there, and bridged to the world of studying and teaching in a religious habit in Long Island, and two missions in Puerto Rico and equally hot Texas. She was one of the first to take the leap to parish work to be with the poor in the Lower East Side of New York, and then twice to the shanty towns, the pueblos jóvenes on the outskirts of Lima, Peru.

She now serves in the nursing wing where the sisters use a floor in a huge Catholic Nursing Home in Queens.

She "buys it…" — the deep belief that God is present in a shared meal.

Her journey is not naïve; she knows only too well the attempts at stifling of the Spirit of female and male congregations and their service with and among the poor. Her still-warm accessibility is drawn from her prayer and yes, her own wounds and those of the women she has lived with. A certain youthful, inquisitive and energetic support for new missions is clear. She wants real people to feel at home in the Church, a daunting job as the gap really does exist with the poor and uneducated and the more formal ways of dioceses and religious corporations.

My first memory of her: a slim, then black-haired, lively and attractive woman with a warm smile, was in the vestibule of a large, daunting Church. She was spending time on an equal platform with grizzled, aging women putting small price tags on religious statues, "to help the community." Afterwards we ate pierogies at an Eastern European place. Leave it to her to choose a poor simple place. She liked beer that day and wine now. Her eyes still light up with a youthful glistening and sparkling of hope.

As with all of us, COVID has crashed into her life now, as she tries to protect the already ill, aging sisters in the nursing floor from further decline.

Her light of service has not gone out.

She makes retreats on a regular basis – to go deeper. She can be short on words on the phone and keeping a distance from modern technology except for "the job."

To be sure, I have noticed that the youngish smiling, fun-loving look in her face is still very much there, but her voice has also become sharper in its prophecy. This is seen in her knowledge and fighting for the environment. She is also painfully aware of the dying nature of the institutional life of the Church. She knows this self-consuming hunger in both the coldness of Church and climate change can be foreboding cousins at many levels.

The cyclical devastation in both worlds is quite real for her. Although her thin body is being stretched with work with the dying religious sisters in the advanced care nursing home, her vocal, ever-present faith continues. This is clearly not based on the holiness of male leaders, but is fed more from the real witness of her educated religious sisters, the laity, and yes, even some men!

She wishes to abide in the home of Jesus, and she continues to invite others to see and sense that warm, accepting and inclusive invitation. For her—and the fifteen-year-old in a math class — there is no other way.

Although wide-ranging, her pathways have not been circuitous. They have been as straight forward as they can be as they attempt to follow the footsteps of the poor, down-to-earth Son of God. He too had left the small towns of Bethlehem and Nazareth.

She will keeping on walking as long as He still appears at meals with those who see beyond the earthy elements.

Chapter 8

Feisty Mary

She has an internal wit which is inquisitive. Like the Burning Bush inviting the naturally timid Moses, it has not been suffocated.

Beginning in a large farm family in Kilkenny, Ireland, she and two other sisters in her brood intelligently chose a vibrant international group of religious women to do their life-vocation. They began in education, and spread their energetic inclusiveness to engage in justice for women at all levels.

Where did that grace come from? She pipes up and says: "The Holy Spirit, man!"

Certainly, it was not the male hierarchy, and she would admit that with a smirk and a grin. She is not content to become sarcastic or despondent. She centers on her relationship with Lord, and is content to say that life is okay with a thousand friends, both male and female.

Her simple and practical advice about the celibacy and chastity expectation in the lives of religious sisters and priests is: "Have many boyfriends and many girlfriends!" Sister may deny that she has said that, but it does make much sense. Practical experience has taught many celibates that it really is better to spread your living and loving energy around rather than put all your eggs and energy in one basket.

She can be self-deprecating, but not in a terribly negative way. She knows who she is, and is now ready to meet retirement, heads-on and feet-up! All this she does with energy, intentionally so. She is fully determined to do what is right by her co-workers in the kingdom of God. She was glad to hear that one of her primary tasks as a grade-school principal was to decorate schools with flowers. As nature grows, so do the children. How could there ever be schools without flowers??

That makes *SO* much sense, flowers and growth in school hallways. Her common sense is so refreshing. She simply looks at the lack of women in priestly roles and exclaiming, "Like *WHEN*, O Lord, is my Church going to show some common sense? We women can't be all that bad!" She adds with her broad sense of humor, "… and we left Eden a long time ago, but haven't they noticed?"

Her time with Lord is essential to her.

By no means, is the life of the Lord separate from her social gatherings, and also serious and abundant reading. For some unexplained reasons, she is timid of her own writing ability, but not of her charismatic, verbal ability. She clearly talks on the Life of the Spirit in Zimbabwe, Rome, and Saint Louis.

Her own attraction to the Spirit was deepened in her experience of being with the legendary Father Francis MacNutt. While on retreat being led by him in a large cold, drafty religious house, now closed, in working class Staten Island, she learned a lesson of value and newly focused life.

She has shared this teaching at many scenes and times since then. Yes; she had been busy about the "things of the Lord," but now she learned that what mattered was to be busy about the Lord Himself.

In the spirit of the Burning Bush, she keeps things simple and straight-forward.

Is there really any other way?

I hear her answering: "NO, man! NO, woman!"

Chapter 9

Helen Marie Teresa Smith

She deserves it.

Her full correct name.

My Mother.

She died at 67 with cancer of the breast. She had suffered for five years in stoical silence. We were Irish American enough not to use the term "breast." This perhaps sounds silly, but we also never thought she would die.

She was so energetic; who, then, was the "we?"

"We" were my father, whom I was named after; my older brother, a newspaper reporter, and I, then a young Catholic priest working with poor Latinos in Manhattan and the South Bronx.

"We" included others whom she touched with her quick mind, such as the wide-eyed grade school students in an old-fashioned Catholic grammar school. She shined there, as she kept the peace between a progressive religious sister and the VFW pastor. Sister had been arrested for protesting the War in Vietnam at St. Patrick Cathedral no less; one certainly could taste the tension after that.

We included her clear-eyed view of life that also was focused solidly on the realities of family life. That included 43 years of dedicated married Catholic life to a New York Fire Department husband with ever-changing work hours. She certainly followed the rules of worship and modesty, but also giggled at home in the kitchen if the homilies were not making sense.

This balanced view of religion and its possible importance is seen in this vivid memory. I had come home to the apartment house after blessing one of the deceased neighbors at a grave site. The person who died was the saint of the parish, and the hearing sister of two deaf mutes whom my parents often visited one floor above them in the apartment house. I had said some prayers at the cemetery at the request of the relatively young parish priest. But, on this a warm day, I did not say all of them that were in the prayer book. She piped up: "Don't worry, Jimmy; all that folks want by that point is to get to the restaurant and drink!"

Mom loved her God, her Jesus, and was totally fascinated by her Liberal and Reform Jewish neighbors. She was intrigued by those who worshipped on Saturday, as our day was Sunday. This Catholic mother knew clearly that college for the children was the unifying element in the laundry room and beyond. All religions were okay, as long as you practiced.

This Irish American woman knew religion was important so "as not to kill each other in the apartment house!" When I have used that line from Chinatown to working class suburbia, folks laugh.

She was on to something, something deep and life-giving and wider than the walls of her small kitchen.

Faith was in her heart, but it was not to be confused with superficiality nor phoniness nor being churchy. Her eyes told stories without words; they could pierce with warmth, glistening laughter, and healthy anger. She was a whirlwind of energy and action, and could laugh at herself and the foibles of her world, the church ladies, and her family members.

Her relationship with the priests in the parish was rooted in awesome respect for "the hands of the priest." He could bless the bread and wine and make it special. I wrote once in a self-evaluation in my many years in the seminary that "My mother says that we respect priests but we do not put them on a pedestal." The modern, progressive seminary professor thought that was good theology.

The priests needed that healthy respect. They would say: "When Mrs. Sheehan looked at you with her clear blue eyes, she would look right through you."

True.

She was looking for what made you click, what made you feel you had dignity, what did you really believe. Mom was looking for nothing less than your soul.

Helping others to feel they had dignity was in direct response to her being the daughter of Irish American immigrants. Her parents came from different ends of the immigrant experience.

Her tall mother, an orphan, came over in steerage on an unnamed boat. Her beloved father came over in second class, as his brothers did not want him to be traumatized by an already hard voyage. They met working for a large convent of religious women. She was a domestic; he was a chauffeur. She had a big brother who entered the seminary and left two years before ordination.

The Holy Spirit came to her heart one day in her first job. She was taking a bus in Yonkers, and she figured out at 19 that if she were to be a mother of boys she would raise them in freedom. There was nothing in her background to enable her to be a freedom-giver, but she delivered on freedom quite well, 95% of the time.

Her mind was a formidable force. She had won "The Cup!" for general excellence from her Catholic high school, but broke the nuns' hearts as no girl nor neighbor whom she knew went to college. Life has its curves, as the overwhelming majority of students in my colleges are now women, often daughters of immigrants.

Her knowledge was not bookish, even in a home of avid readers and her husband, who read two newspapers a day. She was very clear that schedules were important, but only if you did not tell her younger son, me, that there really was an expectation on eating on some semblance of organized Western time.

To eat as a family was sacred, but that could be at anytime.

No; she has not died, at least not for me.

She tells me to be myself each morning, and very clearly and firmly: "Not to play the game!"

She loved her God and could see the Almighty as part of Church, but even more as an indicator of what could be in life. She welcomed newcomers to whatever corner of life that they found themselves in; her world was both small and yet very expansive.

No; life does not have to make sense. I can hear her giggling that a parish is like life. She smiled as she declared that: "You muddle through it!"

Much truth there.

Maybe her life was like swimming, which she loved, and honestly never was that good at. She would enjoy letting go, even though she had a tight bathing cap on her small head.

She also had trouble breathing at the end.

In a small hotel pool on Cape Cod, Massachusetts, her shortness of breath made it impossible for her to swim to the other end. The tears were silent that late afternoon when we left the pool together. They are now only really expressed when I pray, or try to pray. The "groans of creation" are felt when I hold hands at the Our Father with immigrants, just as I once held her own small hands at a Holy Thursday Eucharist in the Northwest Bronx. I was a senior then in high school, and we were in a gym in the Bronx that we used as church.

Eventually, she would whisper over long distance phone calls that we had a special closeness.

She is right, and the whispers still speak volumes across the thin space.

Chapter 10

Margarita

Determination.

Determination herself huffed and puffed on the way to the top floor of an old-fashioned Catholic grammar school in the changed Bronx. Meet the teacher, *la profesora*, with eyes that saw it all. She was born a teacher. Even when she wore an orange dress for a full recital in a leadership type school in the Philippines, she felt that she would be teaching as a lifestyle and a job somewhere. Music and its precision is tied to math, and that is how I met her. I never knew her as a music teacher, but her voice with an accented lilt and sparkling eyes could lead one to hear a bit of *The Sound of Music* with Julie Andrews..

Well...perhaps that's a bit of a stretch. However, somewhere between Nigeria in the Muslim section and the seedy Bronx she performed as a leading educator —and an unabashedly religious one at that.

Never apologetic for her sense that God was as close as a fresh flower, she has plowed through life's experiences belying both her age and relatively young widowhood. Her deep dignity touched the hearts of many mature believers, and those who wanted to be mature.

Friendship with her was never a straight path; she had seen and felt so much in her journeys, including that of her three distinctly different adult children. God and her formidable mind were two real toll-plazas one had to stop at to get to know her soul.

Both were important for her.

She cried at the slipping away of celebratory cultural ties from Asia that made religion not separate from life, but more of a lyrical dance. That pushed the pathway on the rocky streets of the Philippines to a new, but always dignified way of doing things. In many ways she was a step out of line with the crass and often loud North American culture.

She certainly felt uneasy at the superficiality of many of the male clergy. Up until her early '50's she did her jobs of family, school and prayers apart from the "UP's" – "You People"—as she called the clergy. As a serious student of the Catholic faith, she did not let the shenanigans of those in the Inner Circle get in her way of trying to do God's will with little ones. Saying that, she never let on publicly her frustration on the silliness of having to teach Church History in the 8th grade—before the students even knew about Jesus.

However, there are many sides that make her memorable. She took cooking seriously—and always wanted to cook for more people. She never minded working over a hot-stove in a soup kitchen, as she tried to understand her workers with different accents.

She was Eucharistic in the most profound sort of way. She often sorely disappointed when the culture in the states was too busy to say "thanks" in any formal or informal way.

She valued deeply the Sacramentality of Friendship. The dedicated Benedictine Sisters who taught her travelled from the disciplined world of Germany to the blossoming land of the Philippines. They had taught her that "Sacraments are an outwards sign created by God to give grace." She fundamentally knew deep in her heart that friends were to be cared for and nurtured. She was able to receive the gift of friendship in a cautious and dignified way. She would not be publically demonstrative of affection in her dealings outside her family – and probably her God.

God for her touches the mind, but only if it first goes through her heart. That is where the music comes in, particularly from her favorite: the romantics. Her world was not to be confined to the four corners of her home, but was to include her frequent trips to other lands, spirituality courses, and yes, "restaurants with ambience."

Her passion for the holy could be perceived as being pushy at times, especially by people whom she cared for. She did not mind getting lost with directions visiting hospitalized friends of her family in an old station wagon, nor did she stop loving even in the non-polished, incomplete tension at the edges of friendship. Then again, there was an aura of loneliness that was present even with her friends.

Was this an area reserved for God, alone?

Probably, but the artist inside of her really will not give us a black-and-white answer on that.

Mystery was the original word for sacrament.

She would be comfortable with that; God's lively love mysteriously uplifting the classroom in any neighborhood or corner of the world. She is no Julie Andrews, as she struggles to choose to walk with a cane. Her eyes though, even as they age, still do glisten with Faith at the God of Musical Beauty.

Let her intense interest in real education play on.

Chapter 11

Carolyn

Why are straight-forward people so confusing?

Take Carolyn, transplanted to now three states after being raised as the youngest in a Russian Slavic American working class home in the Northeast. You may think that she would settle down as the well-trained librarian, who is using all her digital skills to settle into some niche into some part of the school system. Or to use her love and capacity in languages to become a star in the service industry directed to new immigrants. Or probe even deeper into her very religious roots to be content with at least one manifestation of Christianity.

Her faith is an exhilarating constellation from so many bleeding crosses in her home of origin to a blazing feminism that sees the need for authentic change by the male hierarchy now—before later.

No; staleness and inertia or a self-satisfied sarcasm is not what is happening at all.

Her focused energy pushes her and pulls her to confront the very incongruities in the actual institutions that she wants to serve. For a quiet, surprisingly small woman, she is always on some kind of crusade, like Don Quixote fighting the windmills of the status quo. The image of her body jumping out of her skin can be valid. Whether it be in jeans, a skirt, or a pantsuit, she cannot sit in one spot for a long time. Her eyes dart; she wants to know what is happening with ladies' conversations in a deli, as well as the philosophies that lie behind and below institutions of control.

She is into women's rights—but is indignant at what she sees as infringement of that basic area of reform by other issues (e.g. transgenderism.) She teaches high school enough to see the effects of "senior lesbianism," and rejects the tendency to exalt experimentation over evidence of healthy practices.

She lives and almost dies for research and the evidence basis behind all attempts at social reforms. She is the kind of woman whom you want at a meeting, as she will be a strident voice on the side of the underdog, usually the immigrant. Carolyn is also the kind of woman whom you do not want at a meeting as she challenges trendiness to the often bitter end.

Her eyes can be sharp; she wants to focus on the truth and not be diverted by either power-games or circus-style political correctness.

Her husband sees her drive as coming from the stars. There is definitely a multi-level approach to life's curves that bounce through her quick and long e-mails. She does value her articulate ability addressing the administration of schools on issues that they may not be that interested in. The image is that the men have left the world of the campus a long time ago, and what is left is some kind of woman's voice crying out in the wilderness. Her voice is a lonely singular one –a cross between John the Baptist and the small sycamore tree climbing Nicodemus. She intends to see the spiritual in the world's mess that she knows only too well through studies.

Is she carrying an empty suitcase of unfinished plans for a super-engaged learning and a modern environment? Does she trip over the need to have students and administrators to still be able to spell and do the basics? Does she care whether the larger world will listen to her – ever? Apparently not.

What is true suffices for her; she will go out of her way to research and explain her views – even at times in a fiercely, articulate way. She is playing for keeps, with a wild brand of fire to help create new ways, particularly for young women. Yet, she is rooted in the old and is afraid when all politicians and so-called educators of all stripes give themselves an image as agents of change.

Full of paradoxes, she wants to go where her deeper energy—and yes, her stars lead her.

Will she ever settle down?

Probably not.

Her almost ruthless research ability is grounded in her need and desire to find the truth –or is that truths?

Chapter 12

Erica

Fresh, bold, vivacious ... changing images of herself and her dress nearly every day. For some reason, after her fourth outfit with different earrings in four days to my office, I simply said: "I look at your soul –and that is good."

As strange – if not esoteric as it may sound — she understood that.

Her eyes yelled out for acceptance and freedom. She was going to be someone different than the statistics around a Puerto Rican Latina woman serving as a guardian of her younger cousins between two harsh apartments on different sides of Burnside Avenue in drug-infested neighborhoods.

Her heart reaches out to a God who is realistic. This is a God who would not judge folks involved in relationships outside the standard expectations of a rigid Church becoming more rigid. Legalism is not an outfit that she would ever wear— nor would her God from the islands.

That stance is not culled from late adolescent rebellion. No;

she has really invited Mary, the Virgin, to accompany her in her often bewildering relationships with Latino machos, her family, and even other unattached immigrants. She knows Mary to thrive as a woman who is a personal friend of the poor still, despite it all. No plastic statue for her; she opts and dances with the real thing: a young Mary.

Her deep brown eyes have seen a lot—too much for someone in her twenties. She knows only too well of the damaging possibilities of drugs, beer and incarceration — even in her strong family.

She knows her roots, both in Spain and in the Taino natives and their rejection of the mentality of their colonizers. She is in touch with that rebellion for the sake of being herself.

Her favorite room at the college was the library. She went there to clear her mind—and she was transported from the streets that were so loud and unfulfilling.

Her energetic body and need for independence brought her to other men and other religions. She kept her distance from going too far with her attractive body, as she sadly saw how many in her cohort had left the college due to pregnancy. Bronx people are in touch with consequences; well, at least she is.

I always liked meeting her family, including her papi, with whom we shared a beer with in a hot brownstone in the South Bronx. She had passed through enough silly exams and arrogance of some teachers who had looked down their noses at brown-skinned student-teachers. Her cohort wanted to be educators affecting the future. She had become her dream: a certified bilingual middle-school teacher.

She fights intelligently to stay with her dream. To keep her integrity, she has bounced among schools with dominant principals. The administration of many types of service agencies is often forced to be concerned about other realities than the dangers of the projects and the hazardous broken homes from which the children come from. She wants to make a difference in children's lives. This dynamic Puerto Rican still exhibits the fire of the island. While aware of the real limits of her family, she does not buy the American Dream lock, stock and barrel. Somehow, and somewhere, there is a refuge for her soul, which no one has touched nor damaged, try as they may. Erica has not stopped looking.

For all her professional demeanor, her heart breaks when another relative of the school-aged children gets sent to jail, which is the graduate school of ignorance, learned victimization, and violence. She learned well the words "access to resources," and she applies that concept to reality. This student, now turned mature woman, has no problem in reminding, distant monolingual monsignors that is what the Church exists for: the poor and the unnamed. They are as important as the scholarship winners and the want-to-bees.

Her desire to draw strength from padres as non-cultic priests and hopefully, healthy father-figures, is a blessed two-way street for all involved.

She wants to throw herself into the wisdom of the ages, to receive the good news of acceptance, dignity and real education. Her educational work is to apply that spirit to the cold, dusty dangerous corners of her barrio. This teaching is not a job for her; it is her life.

One night I saw her get into an Uber car service, which she could pay for, driven by another adult student. On the next corner, there was an unruly mob of teenage girls cursing up a storm.

The contrast was painfully evident.

This feisty, high energy Latina woman was not above the street-gang of undisciplined and unfocused anger.

She just surely was not going to be kept there.

Chapter 13

The Future of the Other

This thirteenth chapter might be significant.

We are crossing the shallow Rubicon from observant short silhouettes, stories of women, both living and physically deceased, to the substantial issues. Can we have more freedom-producing religion and philosophy for Catholic Churches and other religions to ordain women?

Of course, it is easier to try to shut down all commentary on ordaining disciples who are women. In matter of fact, some clerical monolithic, clerical leaders would say quite strongly in foreboding tones of apodictic power that one is NOT even to think about such wild ideas. The blatant reality is that the Janes and Maries of our lives cannot be ordained, certainly not liked the trusted carriers of religious traditions, such as the Teddies and Peters in the public life of ministry.

Regarding the public ordination of female priests, the safer way is to hide behind the skirts of tradition rather than deal with ever-changing world of gender roles. Just last night I saw on national TV a woman line-judge at the Super Bowl, but I know she is not to be considered for the life-giving role of merciful confessor and reconciler for broken, hurting faithful waiting for redemption through the Sacrament of Reconciliation. Perish the thought!

I see and have read about the noble sacrificial work of firewomen in my Dad's old job in the New York Fire Department. However, they are not to use oils on the foreheads of emerging teen leaders and candidates in Confirmation programs in parishes. Our earthly mothers of all cultures and stripes have given us food in all seasons of life's journey. They are still sadly are forbidden to lead prayer or preside at the Table of the Lord in Eucharist, or receive a babe into the family of the Church.

Why these rules still exist is for other folks in the distant, opaque corners of the Church's constellation to ponder. However, at what cost are we missing the God-given qualities of women to present a different face of God to a lonely planet?

Let us keep it simple—and proclaim the basics.

How can we not use Emma's courage; my mother's exuberance for the sacredness of the mind; Ann's and Jo's radical respect for the independence of their children; Ellen's joyful confidence in the presence of the Higher Power; Margarita's disciplined confidence to teach the Ways of the Lord in season and out; Maggie's awesome and breathtaking grace to create new roles for herself and other women; Feisty Mary's sense of universal call; Margaret's need to return to the quiet center; Anne's blessed choice to stay pure as she can and stay away from the traps of power; Carolyn's straight-forwardness in articulating truth; and Erica, as she is still writing afresh the dreams of an independent woman like Mary who still whispers "Yes" to new life.

The food is on.

While the way we eat might be different, our earthly mothers would certainly not want antiquated reasons to delay and try to block what is really life-giving.

Acknowledgments

Although book-writing as a ministry appears as a solitary enterprise, creativity really does involve a community of support and realistic encouragement.

I sincerely want to thank Susan Perkins of **colperresearch.org** for her spirited, Christian enthusiasm for this project. How could I forget the thoughtful and admittedly long critiques with reflections of my initial wanderings by Mr. Mike Wierzbowski, former editor of our college literary magazine from the last century.

I also wish to express gratitude for Mr. Marco Gallo of Maryknoll's Art Department, who extended his visual skills to the work of this literary mission. To be sure, I was also edified by my brother, Tom Sheehan of Boston, for his professional concern on this important topic.

"May those who have ears to hear use them…" (Matthew 13:9)— and open their hearts in our post-9/11 and now COVID worlds,

With Less Fear of Change,

Peace,

(Fr.) Jim Francis Coy Sheehan, Jr.
June 30, 2021, The Feast of the Roman Martyrs
On My 42nd Year of Priestly Ordination

Printed in Great Britain
by Amazon

82762803R00048